UNDER A POLICEMAN'S KNEE

Social Justice Poetry and poems about
facing adversity plus more

Rick Ward

authorHOUSE

AuthorHouse™
1663 Liberty Drive
Bloomington, IN 47403
www.authorhouse.com
Phone: 833-262-8899

Published by AuthorHouse   03/29/2023

ISBN: 979-8-8230-0243-1 (sc)
ISBN: 979-8-8230-0244-8 (e)

Print information available on the last page.

This book is printed on acid-free paper.

The United States Tennis Association's National Community Service Award winner

Rick Ward

Rick Ward, of Sacramento, California has done more to grow the game of tennis over the last 20 years than nearly anyone. From "Tiny Tots," to seniors, to wheelchair players, to NJTL, he is a tireless and selfless promoter of tennis. As the Tennis Director for the City of Folsom he has built the program from scratch to over 4,000 participants. He has received a Resolution of Commendation from the Mayor of Folsom for his efforts creating one of the top recreational programs in the country.

Rick is the director and founder of the River City Tennis Circuit, a tournament program that also includes team tennis leagues, flex leagues, and other social events for people of all ages. It has grown to become the largest tournament circuit in Superior California. Rick has directed approximately 270 tournaments in his career. He has taught over 20,000 lessons working for both public agencies and private tennis clubs. He has taught many high school players with 20 going on to compete collegiately. A great majority of these students were beginners when Rick began working with them. More than 70 adult and junior students combined have won at least one tournament with Rick as their coach. Rick was also the coach of the USTA's Northern California Player of the Year from 1995 through 1997. He also coached a couple of high school championship teams in the mid 1980's.

Rick is an inspiration to the general public offering every type of tennis program available and is one of the leading promoters of team tennis in the country. His work promoting team tennis was acknowledged at a dinner ceremony in Sacramento with Billie Jean King a few years ago. He is always on the cutting edge when it comes to offering new and exciting programs. One example is a Davis Cup style tournament for adults and expanding the NJTL by creating the Sierra Foothill League for beginning juniors. He has also expanded Play Tennis America, a free lesson program to include flex leagues for the participants which has kept new beginning players involved in our sport.

Rick has accomplished all of this while overcoming an arthritic condition that has left him with an artificial wrist and nerve damage as a result of the implant. He has had to learn to use the racquet with three fingers to continue to teach. He also had to learn to walk again after being hit by a car as a pedestrian trying to push a stalled car off the freeway. His efforts would be amazing for a physically healthy person, let alone someone who has physical obstacles to overcome.

Rick's motivation is to bring new players into the sport and is not based on financial rewards. He has raised money for the disabled by personally holding serve-a-thons where he once served tennis balls for 24 consecutive hours on one occasion, and then 32 continuous hours on another.

Rick Ward is "tennis" in Sacramento. He has done more than anyone for the park districts in the Sacramento area. As the Head Pro at three different tennis clubs he has resurrected two dying programs and built another from the ground floor creating the largest indoor tennis program in the area.

Contents

Under a Policeman's Knee

In Covid times of lonely death
a black man took his final breath
four cops in all brought on the strife
compelled George Floyd to beg for life
his final words were I can't breathe
under a policeman's knee
cops sworn to serve, sworn to protect
an oath some treat with bold neglect
the badge some wear has lost its shine
dripping with their racist slime
under a policeman's knee
Chauvin charged with murder one
wants the charge dismissed
no remorse for what he's done
no empathy exists
under a policeman's knee

Breonna Taylor EMT, killed inside her home
this unarmed black was innocent, still she died alone
no knock warrants, deadly weapons, often overkill
raiding quiet homes showing force provide police a thrill
several cops broke through her gate
she felt their guns, died from their hate
under a policeman's knee
no cameras worn claimed the cops
that kept us unaware
but photos showed there were a few
showed a lack of crime scene care
a bloody scene of bullet holes
shell casings on the ground
seems they were moved deceitfully
in a different place were found
under a policeman's knee
cops names first kept from public view
authorities protecting blue
cowardice for all to see
when there's no transparency
Kentucky cops still not charged
for their heinous crime
this scene played out across the land

"continued"

far too many times
under a policeman's knee

A thin skinned cop
blew his top
when a black man
turned and walked away
cops with ego's can get hot
when they're disobeyed
seven shots to Blake's back
his kids watched in disbelief
Jacob's life now off the track
can't walk or find relief
under a policeman's knee
to protest cop brutality
Kenosha tried it mournfully
white militia found their spot
joined the cops and more got shot
dying, under a policeman's knee

when cops break the law
by gunning down blacks
respect all but gone
may never come back
so Colin took a knee
any change since Rodney king
apparently not anything
racism, a hate song that just never ends
when sung by white cops
they're no longer our friends
black lives have to matter
these shootings must end
all white police
should make a black friend
systemic problems our country must fix
should all blend together, a tolerant mix
this is not something
that should have to be taught
should not be a war
that should ever be fought
every precious black life
should know they are free
not a single one dying
under a policeman's knee

2

Sea World Slavery

Orca killer whales
smartest creatures in the sea
displaying complex rituals
from the dolphin family
patrolling seas for centuries
twelve pound brains evolved with time
second only to the sperm whale
four times the size of mine
two different types of Orca's
share Pacific coastal seas
these Residents and Transients
are as different as can be
don't get along in open seas
or in Sea World Slavery
Orca families, female ruled
survive by processing sounds
emitting signals with rebound effect
echolocation is how meals are found
in tightly-knit families
males rarely stray from home
stay very close to mother
don't like to be alone
they navigate and socialize
with whistles, clicks, and groans
Sea World Slavery
produces mostly painful moans
can live as long as eighty years
in our planet's seas
lives are cut by more than half
in Sea World Slavery
Sea World's claim of longer life
due to veterinary care
is a view and a claim
marine biologists don't share
can swim one hundred miles a day
when free in salty seas
forced to live in concrete bathtubs
that's Sea World Slavery

"continued"

Sea World whales live in distress
don't have another choice
they break their teeth biting gates
only way to have a voice
limp dorsal fins on Sea World whales
a sad sight every day
this certain sign of inner stress
not seen in ocean play
Hugo's choice was suicide
banged his head on concrete walls
possibly he gave his life
to hasten Sea World's fall
with speed boats, planes, explosives
and large three-acre nets
Orca's kidnapped from their mothers
hearing cries they won't forget
lifted from the sea and forced into slings
frightened Orca's learn what confinement will bring
our turn styled money helps to fund the chase
hunting for Orca's adds to Sea World's disgrace
some Orca's don't survive the chase
what does Sea World money do
they're cut wide open, filled with rocks
then sunk, anchored out of view
if our kids were taken, never seen again
do they make the choice to be their captor's friend
that's the choice for these whales
it's no surprise they're mad
their lives will never be the same
Sea World's taken all they had
Orca's have no record attacking humans in the sea
the same cannot be said in Sea World Slavery
captive whales pose a threat
once no longer free
the Blackfish film made us aware
Tilikum has killed three
some trainers never told
others told too late
of many dangers they would face
Sea World blames them for their fate

Arden Park

Brought to life with children's laughter, the trees stand tall
overlooking their innocent play, protecting them from tomorrow's call
Play Children Play!
Young lovers meet in private retreat
to enjoy tender moments that are touching and sweet
Love Children Love!

Baseball diamonds waiting for play
share center field with soccer kids
trying to reach their goals today
Dream Children Dream!

A two-sided tennis wall twenty feet high
bouncing balls back to children
who may swing and miss, but at least they try
Swing Children Swing!

An empty basketball court left alone feeling blue
isolated children can feel lonely too
Cry Children Cry!
Children flying from swings to the ground
taking risks to find that courage is found
Leap Children Leap!

Tennis courts with broken nets
ignored by swimmers who'd rather not sweat
Swim Children Swim!
Children climbing steps to a tall twisting slide
winding down curves on life's unknown ride
Climb Children Climb!

Little Leaguers with baggy uniforms that just don't fit
parents watching and playing even while they sit
No Parents No!

Arden Park, a Sacramento playground surrounded by homes
that have gathered together for several generations
all to hold the yesterdays that couldn't live for the moment
Live Children Live!

A Symphony of Sound

Ocean waves of white capped foam
rush toward the waiting shore
then turn around, go back out
coming back to play some more
    Tapestries of Sound!

This encore of sound's worth heeding
It's chorus line repeating
a lilting lullaby caressing sand
gentle music conducted by nature's hand
    An Orchestra of Sound!

The calm swaying rhythm of soulful waves
drawn to shores of a sand-filled stage
waves follow in cadence as if by choice
while Seagulls land to add their voice
    A Diversity of Sound!

A sharp-eyed lighthouse manages to keep
melodic waves working together in tune
providing direction for overconfident waves
who would rather showboat, than croon
    A Conductor of Sound!

A crescendo of chaotic waves
pound and crash against sharp rocks
like drum symbols recklessly playing
to the mournful cries of Seagulls flocked
stubborn weather not obeying
    An Eruption of Sound!

After storm clouds pass
dancing waves slow
producing soft notes
and a smooth flow
for working fishing boats
    A Change of Sound!

Whistling winds from ocean caves
add to the sound of metered waves
the ebb and flow of pulsing tides
uncover what our oceans hide
it pulls together what we've found
    The Ocean's Symphony of Sound!

Never Second Place

A dark bay beauty, some called her black
Her talent revealed once on the track
Flying from the gate quickly to the lead
Fans and all horses in awe of her speed
At every point of call in every single race
She was always in first, never second place
Coming down the stretch skimming the rail
Waving goodbye with the swish of her tail
So far in front at the end of each race
Took a long time to see the horse in second place
Records broken or equaled every time she raced
Ten races unbeaten, never second place
She took the filly triple crown, a rare and awesome feat
Beat the Derby winner and her legacy would be complete
The Derby winning horse, a colt named Foolish Pleasure
The difference between them they thought a match race could measure
Fifty thousand in the stands wearing t-shirts and pins
Some read I'm for her, others I'm for him
The battle of the sexes millions watching from home
The queen and king of racing, could a girl take the throne
One jockey rode them both, for this race he'd have to choose
Chose her as the better horse thought she couldn't lose
Calm and collected Ruffian was poised
She didn't seem bothered by all the crowd noise
Anticipation grew as race time drew near
Excited tension but no sense of fear
At the sound of the bell she hit the side of the gate
With her very first stride she sealed her own fate
Her courage and desire got her the lead
No injury could take away her front running speed
She reached the quarter pole in twenty two and change
She was beating the colt, the stars had it arranged
Then one final step and dreams came to an end
Leaving us to wonder why fate wasn't her friend
One trail of hoof prints were all that remained
Of the unfinished race that ended with pain
She wanted to win, still kept on trying
Running in place even though she was dying
Foolish Pleasure carried on and finished the race
As a deafening silence fell over the place

"continued"

Ruffian's photo always taken because she finished in first place
The winner's circle waited but wouldn't see her face
Buried on the infield grass near the finish line
A final fittingresting place, Belmont Park is where she shined
Her soul took wings and carried her to a place where all wounds heal
Now she can reach her destiny without the pain she'd come to feel
In the green fields of heaven a horse runs as if being chased
Why are so many watching? Ruffian is finishing her race

The Plight of the Homeless

Without a home they walk the streets
Looking for a place to sleep
Some will find a makeshift home
A cardboard box and all alone
Under sympathetic skies
Their thirst is quenched when nature cries
They use the roof to catch the rain
Collecting storms to ease their pain
They beg for food to stay alive
A trash can search is how they thrive
Competing for what's thrown away
Friends are never made this way
We must assume their friends are gone
Because a friend would right this wrong
Survival mode is not so fun
Living life on the run
A job loss here, an illness there
Now one set of clothes are all they wear
Entertained at night by watching stars
On the streets by day and dodging cars
Not really seen by those of us
Who turn away and show disgust
Judge them kindly if you must
But you and I will turn to dust
Thou not rich from human birth
God has promised meek the earth
All they own in grocery carts
With teddy bears and broken hearts
A constant fear of cold dark nights
Some cops forget they still have rights
Defenseless targets, easy prey
A mugger's greed could end their days
Lonely walls surround the rich
While poor men cry in tents they pitch
Empty rooms in giant homes
Could be their chance to take the throne
A second chance to start again
Gives us a chance to be their friend
When you give them food to eat
You are washing our Lord's feet
Speak to them you'll give them hope
A little more will help them cope

Closet Doors

Hiding in the closet suffering on their own
They want to come out but will they still be alone
The pain of being different has dropped them to their knees
Begging God to change them with tears and desperate pleas
The closet is no place to hide but where are they to go
Coming out could be suicide if they face a violent foe
For gays to open closet doors they'll need to use their voice
Tell the world they're born that way and never made a choice
When they muster up the courage to look into the mirror
Accepting who they are, let's call them brave and not a queer
When closet doors come open let's hope we see their clothes
And not a body hanging, a victory for their foes
Rejected by family and bullied by friends
Homophobic hate must come to an end
Intolerant air is hard to breathe with limited closet space
Exclusion is what put them there so you don't have to see their face
Ignorance spews from many pulpits and spreads across the land
Fundamentalist pastors uniting with parents throwing out these lambs
Conversion therapy produces only guilt and shame
When there's nothing wrong with them there is no one to blame
The commandment is to love not to judge those gay
We can choose to do that right or choose to disobey
When we vote away their rights by legislating love
We are the ones who need forgiveness from above
Equality for all is an American stance
We should all be entitled to give marriage a chance
To help them open closet doors we can open hearts and minds
When acceptance takes the first step love won't be that far behind

The Silent Victim

He looked right, and sounded wrong
but you were listening to a different song
peer pressure a song, sung with the lie
that popularity comes with just the right guy
rather than listen to the voice inside
you wanted approval and went for a ride
looking forward to fun on this Saturday night
you never thought a kiss would lead to a fight
you thought saying "no" would loosen his grip
the only sound he heard was your dress as it ripped
he thought you were his and wouldn't take less
entitled to you because others said "yes"
the nightmare continues as you see him each day
the campus police don't believe what you say
torn clothes alone won't convict college stars
DNA only proves you had sex in the car
ignorant others will say you were to blame
your provocative dress an invitation to shame
maybe he was drunk, maybe you too
excuses people use then truth becomes skewed
it's too scary to think it really happened to you
so it must be a lie is a "typical" view
what do you get for revealing this "tale"
threats and denial from those posting his bail
not believed, often blamed, you cry to sleep at times
then become a silent victim of our most hidden crime
even if your case ever makes it to court
your past may be displayed as popular sport
often civil court is where your best chance lies
and if you do take a stand, maybe others won't have to cry

Mississippi Blood

Their unbeaten team made the state proud
But dark faces were few in that bigoted crowd
White fans brought confederate flags to football games
Waving proudly their symbols of shame
Flags with 13 stars were red, white, and blue
The large X their signature for having no clue
The civil war fought at a terrible cost
The South carries on as if they hadn't lost
White hoods and robes have been the law for awhile
Hanging black men from trees without any trials
Another black man dreamed of going to school
Mississippi whites screamed that he was breaking their rules
Their governor believed in a segregated state
They burned crosses to show their level of hate
Kennedy stood up for the rights of the few
And a riot ensued in the fall of 62
The Army came in to protect the man's rights
And Mississippi ghosts rose up for a fight
The devil knows how far hate can go
When he joined with the rebels they let the blood flow
With many burning cars and the sound of broken limbs
Mississippi sank so low the South may never rise again
Another civil war fought to keep a black man in chains
All because the South didn't learn from its pain
So look away Dixie land to a time when all are free
Old times there are not forgot, let's hope they'll never be

Hope for the Wrongfully Convicted

a life interrupted, now un-lived
hidden behind a distant heartbeat,
sent away to growing silence
where only quiet ears
can hear a whispered song of hopeful sound,
an anxious tune played
when your abandoned soul's locked away
worried the truth and a Savior may never be found.
Spiritually tapped, you're left strumming desperate heartstrings
pleading with a tired, innocent voice
for God or someone to redeem you from society's sin,
and another eyewitness mistake made once again.
Your guilty verdict rendered by a jury of lighter faced peers
was a quick decision to end unjustified fears.
A racist choice unanimously made
because they couldn't look past your darker shade.
Now you peek through imprisoned steel bars
that tease your weary arms
as you reach through bigoted barriers
straining for stolen freedom that may never be recovered.
It's somewhat like being buried alive
although you're still breathing it's hard to thrive.
All the while similar faces with disappearing smiles
look back at you like dark mirrors,
reflecting memories of segregated abuse, stained with sympathetic tears.
Constantly searching for the long awaited sight of true empathy
you're trying to capture the faintest sounds of wavering hope
by listening for the key that could unlock prejudice from incarcerated minds
and free you from this never ending nightmare.
When your chance for parole finally arrives
They want an admission of guilt but you won't tell a lie
Then a final plea for justice is heard which lifts your damaged heart
a heart revived by the scientific search for truth,
mended by the unselfish efforts of Innocence Project volunteers,
and kept alive by the temporary escape of continuous prayer.
A prayer finally answered with the evolutionary miracle of DNA,
a discovery that could restore your freedom with a resurrected life,
a life to be lived correcting the system that has put so many innocent lives away.

Unfit

Logical fallacies throughout every speech
Crowd doesn't notice, too dumb to reach
Circular arguments, slippery slopes
Hasty generalizations from an ignorant dope
Can't complete a sentence without slurring his words
Having him as President is more than absurd
Mistaken words that still persist
Using words that don't exist
Station for nation and Nars for Mars
Sounds like he came from the nearest bar
Addicted to his verbal gaffes
Children listen then must laugh
Language flaws for all to see
Fails the test linguistically
Experts in this speaking field have all said the same
His repetitive vocabulary is limited and lame
Academic discourse for this man a dreadful terror
Hidden transcripts will reveal a brain that's full of error
Speaking academically he's unable to compete
To get in school and stay in school this man had to cheat
For him a televised political debate
Is a way to spread misinformation and hate
Every time he takes the stage
Cannot hide his hateful rage
The only skill he does possess
To divide us all from happiness
His supporters have to know
His constant sniffling comes from blow
Getting high coming down one day he may fall
From Sudafed and coke and snorting Adderall
Because of drugs he cannot sleep
That's when he writes his racist tweets
The thought of Vietnam made him piss his pants
Typical of bunker boy are his constant rants
Woodward tapes reveal his hate
From those words he can't escape
Also show that he knew
Covid not from states in blue
Treats women as his property
Assaulting them unlawfully

"continued"

Not at all a businessman
Bankruptcy is his only plan
Six times in all but saved by dad
Owing millions, millions mad
Tax records show this man has failed
Some will say should be in jail
Promises he never keeps
Just a wolf that preys on sheep
Contractors left without a cent
Because he's always overspent
Ruined families in this land
Scottish people know his brand
Sending troops to break up peace
Supports black killings from police
Telling states you must get tough
And treat protestors very rough
Fake news unneeded with this man
His mouth will tell you where he stands
His crimes against humanity
Are seen by all repeatedly
Open up go back to school
Let people die his golden rule
Told the churches open up
So many sick who drank that cup
Touted Hydroxychloroquine
And people died because of him
Insecticides his other cure
North Texans sick who took that cure
Some give support in spite of him
Others do because of his him
Either way they must be lost
And clearer minds will pay the cost
Ignored the science, people died
While Fauci made a valiant try
To live his life without a mask
Covid may take him to task
Saw the virus as a hoax said it would go away
Deciding not to wear a mask leads other men astray
The Tulsa rally was a joke there's not much else to say
Their governor was a fool now has a price to pay
This white house lodger and proud draft dodger
Wants to hide behind a wall
Helps to understand why this fearful man

"continued"

Would not answer country's call
All soldiers are "suckers and losers"
According to this man
He sees them gaining nothing
For their service to this land
this lunatic lacks bravery
And dreams of days with slavery
He knows how to crack the whip
Send in the troops to hurt black lips
A narcissist, a sociopath
No empathy but full of wrath
Fits all criteria to be diagnosed as sick
Shrinks for years have studied him
They know what makes him tick
He is the world's most dangerous man
Agreed by docs across the land
A ticking time bomb that will blow
His small explosions not for show
You gave him power to release
An arsenal not wanting peace
Undiagnosed as a kid his ability to learn
Aides say his attention span is of great concern
Memo's longer than a page are too tough for him to read
Ignores them at our peril and why he can't succeed
Cannot process information that could be vital to us all
His unbelief in climate change threatens one and all
He didn't know that Israel was in the Middle East
Thought we beat the British because our Air Force was a beast
Airplanes not invented yet but said were in the sky
Reveals the man an idiot, addicted to his lies
His knowledge of the simplest things so low it's off the charts
But he lies to us all and tells us that he's smart
If you tell a lie and tell it long enough
America is full of dumb and will believe this stuff
18,000 lies in the last 1,200 days
If you want to have a cry, fact checking is the way
His Administration's instability is a troubling sign
Over 400 people have been fired or resigned
If you disagree with him you probably will be fired
Once he knows you're smarter you probably won't get hired
His actions are predictable in great times of stress
Divert attention from himself so his faults are not addressed
This virus was too much for him and did not disappear

"continued"

With 200,000 dead supporters should be crying, yet they cheer
When he stands in front of church with bible upside down
Such a ploy so obvious he comes off as a clown
Only the deluded dumb could think this con man's real
His disregard for others leaves no capacity to feel
Innocent boys were the Central Park five
Still this man didn't want them alive
His unaccredited university
Was a fraudulent absurdity
Those scammed had their say
Courts behind them made him pay
Incapable of leading he's unfit for the job
He could take you to the bank unless it's one he's robbed
Dependent personality, a disordered inability
To make decisions comfortably or take responsibility
His EPA is killing bees, his pesticides cause disease
Roundup causes cancer, courts have backed that claim
Insisting that it's safe he has to share the blame
He did away disclosing, civilians killed by drones
No accounting for mistakes leaving families all alone
He diverted pay and pensions for our country's vets
For a racist border wall that we should just forget
Stoking racial bigotry claimed that terror crossed the border
Just another sign of his delusional disorder
Data from our border guards does not support the claim
He should turn away from this and hide his head in shame
Separating families putting children in a cage
Does not seem to satisfy his bigotry and rage
Bigotry continues with Islamophobic tweets
Scapegoats their communities with lies he just repeats
We heard the rhetoric before the Bush war
His fear of Iran is a similar bore
Irrational behavior from a desperate man
Makes dangerous decisions when it comes to Iran
Deemed their military to be a terror threat
Undermined diplomacy and we may get a war yet
Killing Soleimani may seem right to some
But almost got us in a war, what is yet to come
Pulled troops out of Syria, our allies were not pleased
ISIS could rebuild, resources could be seized
Our leadership diminishing all around the world
Instead of global partnerships force may be unfurled
Took the awful step of making weapons with low yield

"continued"

Putting nukes and conflict on the playing field
Tried to hurt Biden with his threat to Ukraine
Instead hurts the world causing misery and pain
Congress did their part when they impeached this man
Still we got nowhere left in right wing hands
Senate members cowardly left the man in place
Leaving blood, death, and tears on our country's face
A man without capacity cannot lead or take advice
If he stays in office, Democracy will pay the price
Maybe a psychopath and narcissist and won't accept defeat
We could end up in the courts or fighting in the streets
He lost before and will lose again
Electoral College his only way to win
For Christians who support this man
I'll leave with one last thing
Younger folks are watching you
It's not your songs they sing

A Child With Courage
(A tribute to children who called the authorities)

Mom went to church with a wave and a smile
Came home in a rage
Been that way awhile
What could it be that made mom change
This once happy woman
With her heart rearranged
Went to church with mom
To see what was wrong
To get a clear answer
Didn't take long
They supported a President, famous for his lies
The lying I thought wrong
fueled their battle cry
The very next day mom left for D.C.
I am doing God's work read the note left for me
Didn't know what that meant
So I turned on TV
In shocked disbelief she was right in front of me
I saw the name of Jesus
On the giant flag she waved
With the mob she shoved a cop who was trying to be brave
A confusing sight to see, insurgents hurting cops
Who tried to do their job
But couldn't make them stop
Fearful for and of my mom
Not knowing what she'd do
How far can someone go with right wing Christian views?
Mom became a terrorist inflicting tears and pain
Would she die for her cause
What did she hope to gain?
Tired of hearing all the hate talk from home
I saw where it took her
So I picked up the phone
It's one thing to listen but something else to see
Mom's hate turning violent
Right wing lunacy
So I called the authorities and turned my mother in
Am I a child with Courage
Or a trader to my kin?

Masks

A broken piece of me
is a broken piece of you
our hearts in altered states
provide some different views

There may have been a time
my needs were number one
with the Covid threat
those selfish days are done

We all must wear a mask
so death can't take its toll
lives are being saved
when together as a whole

Politics be damned
our choice to live must win
when we act together
your mask becomes my friend

When we lower pride
to a place we call half mast
unity flags can be raised
togetherness at last

May look like clowns and robbers
with these masks we wear
we fight a common enemy
should we really care

May only see your eyes
because of masks you wear
but the view I have of you
shows me that you care

If still not choosing me
I'll still be choosing you
providing you protection
from your Covid altered views

Changing Clouds

Humble clouds lingering around
were quiet in the sky
we barely seemed to notice them
as they were passing by

These silent clouds innocent and shy
floated around without much to say
harmlessly they shared the open sky
a myriad of shapes that brighten our day

Now, blue skies dotted with white splashes of paint
have disappeared behind our lack of restraint
if there's an artist above who gave us clouds and clean air
we abused it thinking it would always be there

Thick polluted skies of manufactured smog
choking all white clouds with dirty smoky fog
what's in the air the clouds must breathe
absorbing pain they can't relieve

Once resting like soft white pillows
against a canvas sky of blue
changing now to a darker shade
gusty winds acting as a cue

Aggressive clouds all thinking alike
have joined together and made a choice
before getting loud, lightning will flash
then we will hear their thunderous voice

These newly formed menacing clouds
look like soldiers mounting up together
preparing for war to deliver revenge
with a payload of the worst kind of weather

Pent up contents pouring out
torrents of hail, wind, and rain
angry clouds thrash all about
as if trying to cause pain

"continued"

By forming stronger hurricanes
they're crying out against the treatment of our skies
but unlike us show empathy
with a little break in the middle of the eye

A Colorful Nation

This is not a white country and just never been
Making it so, a xenophobic sin
We have brown sisters and black brothers
We are a nation full of cover
We are the British and the Irish
Peace between them my wish
We are the Dutch, we are the Jews
Red natives here, they're still a few
We are China, we're Japan
Some forgave from Vietnam
We are Cuba and we're Haiti
Few choices left they had to flee
We are Croatia and Ukraine
Coming here to ease their pain
We're Mexico and Canada
Slaves put on ships from Africa
Fought a war to set them free
Still left in chains of bigotry
Created laws to segregate
Brought division stained with hate
The justice lady color blind
Is not what the colored find
Equality is our country's call
Civil rights are for us all
Some are Russian, North Korean
Defecting for their chance at freedom
We are India and Brazil
Skin color fear is with us still
Some have brown eyes and some have blue
Does this difference bother you?
Some whites feel replaced
Stormed D.C. and now disgraced
Imagine how the red man feels
This land of theirs whites came to steal
White hoods always out of place
A rainbow represents our race
Columbus Day we celebrate
But he brought both death and hate
We are France and we are Spain
Why does color cause us pain?
There is a cure for fear of color
Just have to get to know each other

Goodbye to our Guns/Farewell to Arms
(A response to mass shootings and gun violence)

The Sandy Hook killings left families to grieve
Then dealt with crazies who said this can't be believed
Parents losing their children there can be no worse fate
Now enduring denial and gun lovers hate
There is no compassion when empathy dies
But there is the truth despite all the lies
Advertising sways men to their guns
Macho status gained once they have one
Mostly white males with gun addiction
A fearful masculine costly affliction
In whatever city mass shootings occur
The NRA will follow making gun rights assured
Half of mass shootings are men killing their mates
Then sending others to a similar fate
Most mass shooters have a history of abuse
Absorbing hate, beating women, mass killers on the loose
Not every right winger has murder on their list
But most mass shooters are right wing extremists
So many mass shootings, so many lost names
Too few questions asked too few answers gained
Ninety eight percent committed by men
Doing so little our country's sin
Guns deliver courage to commit cowardly acts
Politicians do nothing despite all the facts
We finally must say goodbye to our guns
We're too violent a country to be trusted with one

Farewell to Arms

A win-win proposition, never with guns
There is always a loser when someone's shot by one
The best war won is one we never fight
No mutual destruction, no casualties in sight
The enemy of war is simply war itself
So put away your guns and take care of yourself
When Bambi won't come out to play
Seems we're in season every day
Almost 85 die each day
Because hand guns are not put away
The right to bear arms has caused so much harm
Maybe time to say farewell to these arms

The Life of a Tennis Ball

Before they ever take a bounce
They live in plastic cans of three
Inside of them the pressure mounts
Waiting to see what they can be

Tennis balls are meant to be
Exactly who they are
Blessed with speed and accuracy
They could go very far

They could reach the lawns of Wimbledon
Or courts of clay in France
It doesn't matter where they play
They just want the chance

Even if you've never played
They'll be ready when you do
Waiting for that special day
To show what they can do

Tennis balls are patient
For young and old players too
And just like a special friend
They'll always play with you

They want you to enjoy the game
Tell others that you play
That will help to grow the game
And keep tennis balls in play

Before you ever take a swing
Check out what the ball can do
Tap them up and down
And they'll bounce right back to you

Just like a sprinter
Who needs a race to run
Tennis balls need to play
So they can have their fun

"continued"

I hope it's just as fun for you
When you see what you can do
Practice hard and do your best
The tennis ball will do the rest

The first time flying over the net
Leaves a fuzzy feeling balls don't forget
That makes them want to do it again and again
Tennis balls were made to go for a spin

They enjoy being stroked
By racquets with new strings
It seems to give their bounce
A little extra spring

It's your racquet head speed
That helps the ball go fast
And these larger and lighter racquets
Provide a powerful blast

They love the back and forth rhythm
Not having to stop
It's like bouncing to the music
Of today's hip-hop

The longer the rally
The more they enjoy
Bouncing like a kangaroo
And acting like a toy

On the racquet face, a sweet spot
That feels good to every ball
When it's time to hit your shot
That is where you meet the ball

With no fear of heights
Balls love to be lobbed
And only come down
Because it's their job

Tossed into the air
Waiting to be served
Hit that hard and still not scared
Takes a lot of nerve

"continued"

Backspin, sidespin, topspin
Balls know how to do them all
And will perform them for you
Once you've learned to spin the ball

Depending on the surface
They may leave their mark on court
It's the tennis ball's way
Of adding fairness to the sport

When they're missed into the net
Or mishit with your frame
They will forgive and forget
Not placing any blame

This inner lesson very good
For all who play the game
Leave mistakes in the past
Don't let then turn to shame

Tennis is a game of love, not hate
And balls do not discriminate
They'll play with those who can run
And wheelchair players who roll for fun

To win or lose is not their aim
The ball will treat them both the same
Another lesson's very true
We all must lose a time or two

Balls do feel fear
When tempers flare
Smacked into the atmosphere
They could end up anywhere

If not seen in lost and found
They could start feeling stress
Alone on unfamiliar ground
Deflated by their loneliness

Even if they're ever found
It still could be the end
If their bounce back isn't sound
They may never play again

"continued"

Their tennis lives depend
On how high and long they bounce
They give their all but in the end
Their bounce is all that counts

So when they lose their yellow fuzz
And their speed slows to a quiet buzz
They can still be hit on practice walls
Or from machines as teaching balls

Tennis balls can be taught
To play the baseball game
They can bounce and roll, be hit and caught
They just won't sound or look the same

Because of their devotion
They'll put up with being fetched
Spending time in the sloppy mouths
Of all our family pets

When life has to turn the page
The tennis ball will show its age
Still, lines around their yellow face
Have found a way to be embraced

They've been here for us all our lives
Providing fun and exercise
But to help the sick and seniors thrive
Serves a deeper purpose for their lives

As their tennis lives come to an end
They're helping people walk again
Balls used as wheels, now walkers roll
That's helping others reach their goal

This final lesson's hope for you
When you can't play
Life's still not through

Maybe

Maybe God is energy, this brilliant constant light
Maybe some near death, experience, this warm and soothing sight
Maybe he's a father maybe not a he
Maybe more like mother maybe he's a she
Maybe God is hope because we know our lives will end
Maybe want a hand to hold, an everlasting friend
Maybe God is beyond human understanding
Maybe God is full of love and does no reprimanding
Maybe God is close to us and mankind never fell
Maybe God has empathy and man created hell
Maybe God can't be found in any holy book
Maybe God is better than all religious books
Maybe we can't understand we live by natural laws
Maybe something supernatural could really be their cause
Maybe some put good on something they can't see
Maybe human judgments fail the test of accuracy
Maybe we could think of God as a possibility
Maybe live our lives until we see that reality
Maybe God can be heard in the laughter from our kids
Maybe never call them sinners, be sorry if you did
Maybe when they're young and bound to disobey
Maybe put away the stones, let them live another day
Maybe God can't be found in any one religion
Maybe that just causes hate, unfortunate division
Maybe God is in our hearts, something that we feel
May be appeals to ignorance, no proof that God is real
Maybe God allows our pain without a second thought
Maybe heaven's an apology for all the pain we've got
Maybe God sees our tears and counts them one by one
Maybe there will be no more when our time is done
Maybe God is disturbed by those who hate the gays
Maybe God created gays to be just that way
Maybe God loves sinners and really hates the sin
Maybe just an empty phrase that judges once again
Maybe sin is something from which we all have been absolved
Maybe sin's a concept that we should just dissolve
Maybe we can call it sin when love doesn't win
Maybe there's no need to be born again
Maybe God's the author of our evolution
Maybe won't stop suffering, leaving us to find solutions

"continued"

Maybe we are here to love and see what that creates
Maybe we are here, to eliminate all the hate
Maybe we all have a soul and all our pets do too
Maybe that's a hope in life for some to make it through
Maybe God creates the math that science uses well
Maybe God is the math, maybe time will tell
May be the tree of knowledge holds the secrets we now know
Maybe science is the tree, research methods make it grow
May be the order of creation in the Bible's wrong
Maybe our discoveries have shown this all along
Maybe Bible writers thought the moon had its own light
Maybe they just didn't know the sun's what makes it bright
Maybe not surprised by these Bible writing men
May be their lack of science, more than a little thin
Maybe Bible literalists should actually read their book
May be absurd atrocities will provide a different look
Maybe skepticism should always be in place
Maybe contradictions should have been erased
Maybe violence in the Bible is something God commands
Maybe that kind of God I will never understand
Maybe God's immoral, believes in slavery
May be a sacrificial civil war, with our blood set them free
Maybe we don't need a sacrificial son
Maybe he did die for each and everyone
Maybe saying Jesus takes you where you want to go
Maybe doing Jesus is the better route to go
Maybe some think Jesus was always on the right
Maybe on the left, for social justice he would fight
Maybe Abraham had the will to kill his loving son
Maybe I would say take me, or don't kill anyone
Maybe that is a not a test any God would make
Maybe that is a test that I'd refuse to take
Maybe God caused a flood, warning Noah not to rest
May be a genocidal story, fiction at its best
Maybe women aren't to blame for this claim of mankind's fall
May be a fact without them, we would not be here at all
Maybe fundamentalists should never make our laws
Maybe they just cause more pain, exclusive faith the cause
Maybe women, gays, minorities, are victims of their hate
Maybe some don't think of God when they discriminate
Maybe God does not judge, punish, or condemn
Maybe that controlling thought is what we've put on him
Maybe some can agree on the concept of equality

"continued"

Maybe helping you is helping me, well being's our morality

Maybe TV preachers should be silenced one by one

Maybe they don't need more jets, may be not even one

Maybe exploitation is a TV preacher's tool

Maybe they cause bankruptcy, think the listener a fool

Maybe these faith healers should stop pushing people down

Maybe they just cause more pain and come off as dangerous clowns

Maybe white supremacy is a plague on Christianity

Maybe God is color blind always loving all mankind

Maybe unconditional love means we could never fall

Maybe God has never needed anything from us at all

Maybe there are reasons, we separate church and state

May be if one church got too strong, we could be ruled by hate

Maybe that has happened when Trump became their man

May be there are those of faith who never took that stand

Maybe SCOTUS has become a mostly black robed church of nine

May be the Constitution will sadly disappear in time

Maybe Evangelicals lean politically to the right

Maybe God would say their perspective's lost its sight

Maybe the Quran has something to be taught

Maybe some dismiss it without a second thought

Maybe we can get along without religious thought

Maybe most believe it since that's what they've been taught

Maybe there are many who think they know what God's about

Maybe they should whisper, may be humbled if they shout

Maybe these apologists who think they've known God all along

Maybe God would tell them, you've gotten me all wrong

Maybe there's no evidence that proves that God exists

Maybe some don't care, their beliefs will still persist

Maybe faith is mostly all about emotion

Maybe that is all it takes for unwavering devotion

May be the fact I'm writing this means I'm forever cooked

Maybe doubt has a place when opened eyes do look

Maybe Matthew 25 is the way to live our lives

Maybe the world a better place if that verse becomes alive

Maybe God's a puzzle that we will never solve

May be the puzzle is complete when Jesus got involved

Maybe never judge, those who believe and don't

Maybe there will always be, those who will and won't

Maybe heaven is a place where we have all come from

Maybe the returning trip the greatest hope for some

Maybe we can't say there's God with any certainty

But maybe there will be a day that light will shine for me

In Pain

The problem with this pain
It almost never goes away
And when it starts to rain
I know it's here to stay

It's been around so long
It's now a part of me
Have I done something wrong?
Or is this the way it's meant to be

The ringing of the phone
It really hurts to walk
And still I'm all alone
When I reach the phone to talk

The knocking on the door
I'll do my very best
And limp across the floor
To find again they've left

A very simple task
To tie my tennis shoes
I really hate to ask
It's something I can't reach to do

When I'm in a lot of pain
Sometimes too much to cry
I'll wonder how much does it take
Before you really die

Pain
Has
Found
A
Home

Pain, a constant destructive companion
A persistent shadow I can't seem to abandon
It's beyond my comprehension
Why it demands so much attention

    Pain will grab you when you're unaware
    Just to let you know it's there
    Where and when you cannot tell
    May even strike when feeling well

        Pain has grown to become conceited
        Never thinks it will be defeated
        Like a sociopath who is conscience free
        It won't feel bad when hurting me

            Pain hangs around both night and day
            How long it stays is hard to say
            In my frame it's found a home
            Guess I won't have to live alone

The Ring of Pain

Climbed into the ring of pain
To never leave again
Toe to toe I face my foe
Surviving is how you win

As the rounds of life go by
I'm knocked around the ring
Without a bell to end this fight
The fat gal needs to sing

Life can strike below the belt
But who's to judge the foul
Life has chosen me a foe
And did not provide a towel

Attacking each and every joint
Pain considers me its prey
Although I stand up to this foe
I don't move as fast today

Learning how to take a punch
Cuts and bruises take their toll
Life use to be a bowl of cherries
But my foe just took my bowl

Relentless in pursuit of me
My foe is everywhere it seems
And you can't escape a nightmare
When pain is the reality of your dreams

I've hit the canvas many times
But always seem to rise
To take the blows life's given me
I wear courage as my disguise

With a white coat in my corner
Injecting hope into my veins
I'm addicted to adversity
Making comebacks while still feeling pain

Dust on the Shelf

Football fields seem longer
Baseball fences drift away
Basketball hoops reach higher
This tennis talent just hobbles today
Heroes collect dust
Like trophies on the shelf
To wipe the dust away
I threw away these statues of myself
With one final toss
To build new self esteem
And to free the yesterdays
From the pain of their dreams
When I see old friends
The specks of life still last
In their eyes of yesterday
They recreate my past
Run from their friendship
It's their memories I fear
Even though I turn away
Tomorrow is slow to get here
The dust should have all fallen
With my tears to the ground
But I remember the cheers
And the love from that sound
Memories linger on
With my laurels they sit
The crowd has gone home
Why can't I forget?
It was suppose to be different
I thought God had a plan
Placing my dreams
In these truly gifted hands
The talent I have
Is only given to few
But the gift given me
Might as well been sent to you
My passion for sports
Has now been controlled

"continued"

The disease I have now
Has taken its toll
Swelling and deformity
Have increased the pain
Though some drugs have helped
The dust on the shelf still remains

Arms of Reality

Through dream enchanted hours
I've held you in my heart
Never really wanting
Another day to start

Still, days come by
And as they go
They always tell me something
I already know

Reality is what I see
On your finger everyday
So love is sheltered from my storm of feelings
And must remain that way

I treasure dream filled nights
That I spend alone
For it's the only time
My love for you is shown

The darkness of the night
Brings you close to me
Reality is lost in darkness
Giving way to fantasy

I can hold you in my dreams
But mornings set you free
For the arms of reality
Are not attached to me

A Dream That Can't Come True

The past never brought us together
It seems so unfair
You're future's planned forever
I guess time didn't care

If dreams came true
Then you would be mine
But dreams can't undo
The destiny of time

Time has set you on a course
And given you direction
Now my heart is forced
To hide all this affection

Your vow with time
Must last to the end
So time has helped me find
I can only be your friend

Every time I look at you
I have just one thought
You're just a dream that can't come true
And everything I've ever sought

Remember

When life brings you today
   why live for tomorrow
      remember time is not something you borrow

When life brings you a job
   and opens new doors
      remember the one you closed long before

When life brings you to tears
   and your question is why
      remember my heart is always close by

When life brings your heart to half mast
   because promises have died
      remember the love that you buried inside

When life brings you new love
   and you feel its misplaced
      remember loneliness is no better place

When life doesn't live up
   to what it should be
      remember that life still gave you me

The Handicapped

He'll never learn to dance
Or catch any kind of ball
And never got a chance
To walk or even crawl
His constant friend a chair
That rolls from place to place
Accepting undeserving stares
His smile never leaves his face
He cannot paint a portrait
That might bring to life his soul
But his inner beauty's infinite
To love like Jesus was his goal
He didn't try to hide
The deformities that we all see
My friend looked inside
Love's others as himself and so should we
Some will call him handicapped
But his soul is full of love
He feels the source can be tapped
And points to the sky above

To Catch a Dream

Wanting what you never had
Guess that isn't very bad
But threw away your other life
A loving mother and a wife

To catch a dream
Your vision chased
Was all it seems
Your tongue could taste

Will you arrive
Become a star
Or wonder where
Your children are

Don't you worry
Daddy's home
Even though
You're all alone

Reach the top
Don't look back
Don't ever stop
To seek the love you lack

To catch the dream
Your ego craved
Has left your heart
An aching slave

When dreams are gone
And when you die
They'll write your song with an alibi

Forever

The past took your hand
And walked you down the aisle
When he gave you to forever
Did he greet you with a smile?

Forever made you promise
To trust him till the end
And also gave his promise
To be there in the end

Forever led you to the future
So you gave up yesterdays
When sorrow met you there
Did he tell you he would stay?

Forever hid from you
The pain you'd come to know
But love looked like forever
When he let his feelings show

Forever has a way
Of giving hope, reducing fear
Promising himself to you
With words you hardly hear

Forever kept you in his grasp
When children came along
Now treats you with indifference
Like some forgotten song

Forever lost the will to love
And gave up loving you
Couldn't live up to his promise
He left the loving up to you

Forever can't produce
An everlasting smile
But will take you from your past
And walk you down the aisle

Fading Love

Standing toe to toe
My hands upon your hips
Tears began to flow
Your kiss was fading from my lips

As you pulled away
My heart was beating fast
Love began just yesterday
For you it didn't last

Can you tell me what went wrong?
So maybe I won't hurt so long
As tears are falling from my eyes
Are you content to watch love die?

I can't quite understand
How love just slipped right through my hands
I guess I had a hold
Of a heart turned very cold

As you walked away
You turned for one last look
Just a glance to see
What's left of what you took

Tears still running down my cheeks
I couldn't even speak
Not really knowing why
Fading love just waved goodbye

The Piano Is Not For Boys

Sounds lifting from the keys
   Never tickled my ears
      But I was so hard to please
         In those very early years

To help these students play
   Was my mother's call
      They kept pounding away
         I bought a basketball

Went outside to play
   To escape from the noise
      No, I never learned to play
         The piano is not for boys

Wasn't very long
   Until my gift was uncovered
      Bouncing a ball to their songs
         Their gifts were also discovered

Hey, I'd like to learn
   How to make those keys dance
      But everywhere I turned
         They said there's no chance

I'd just like to see
   If there is something else I can do
      An athlete's what you'll always be
         The piano is not for boys like you

Time

The past is a story
Beginning at today's end
And with each day that comes
The past begins again

The future comes tomorrow
Tomorrows fade into the past
All because our today's
Just can't seem to last

The past meets the future
At the dawning of tomorrow
As yesterday drifts away
Today looks back in sorrow

The past spends its time
Just floating away
As today's blend into yesterdays
Without much to say

Looking to the future
Dwelling on the past
Today seems so neglected
Time just moves too fast

A Silent Telephone

You think you're one of the few
Who love never knew
And spend many nights alone
Next to a silent telephone

You've been a victim of words
That cut down deep
But it seems so absurd
Staying home to weep

Turn on the stereo
And listen to them sing
Wondering when
Your telephone will ring

Turn on TV
And what do you see
A lot of lonely people
Wanting not to be

So what do you say?
Why don't you give him a call?
Afraid to fall in love
Because you couldn't take the fall

Silence can be
Such a very lonely tone
Especially when you're sitting
Next to a silent telephone

I Will Be Here

(For my wife Sue on our anniversary)

I will be here
to live up to the promise I have made to you
and bring out brighter colors when you only see blue

I will be here
to thank those who made you for me
thankful all of this could really be

I will be here
when you feel like being quiet
and still love you when you tell me I should diet

I will be here
when you need to speak your mind
and thank you for ignoring my faults some of the time

I will be here
when the laughter turns to crying
and winning or losing we'll be together trying

I will be here
when you do suffer loss
and share adversity whatever the cost

I will be here
to help you dream again
and be here as your loyal friend

I will be here
when you need to cry on my shoulder
and argue with the mirror when it tells us we're older

I will be here
to feel your beauty inside
thankful that's something that you cannot hide

I will be here
to support what you choose to be
but mostly because there is no place I'd rather be

Shy Little Thing Can Really Rock
(about Courtney Hadwin)

Singing on the UK streets
Found her voice on tired feet
Busking gave her confidence
In front of crowds for merely cents
Dad could drive her on most days
Taught her dreams were made this way
Some don't get the way she grooves
Saw James Brown and loved his moves
You Tube taught her how to dance
Voice Kids gave her that first chance
She came real close and didn't win
But now has fans and made new friends
No, not much for idle talk
But this shy little thing can really rock

Sung "Hard to Handle" on AGT
Oh my God! What did I just see?
Sounds like Janis singing blues
Golden buzzer stunned her too
Confetti then came pouring down
Cheers of love flowed all around
She told the world it's tough to talk
But this shy little thing can really rock

Born to be a rock and roll child
Unleashed to sing "Born to be Wild"
"River Deep, Mountain High"
Tina's song she had to try
"Papa's Got a Brand New Bag"
Thought her take was not a drag
Like a lion on the stage
Rock and Roll unlocks her cage
Although she finds it tough to talk
This shy little thing can really rock

Pandemic came and life slowed down
Learned guitar while sitting down
I most like to watch her move
Still has much she wants to prove

"continued"

She'll reach for stars beyond the moon
Hope she's the star that's shining soon
She might find it tough to talk
But this shy little thing can really rock

Through AGT we got to see
Sixth place is not her cup of tea
I hope you saw what I could see
A rock star's what she's got to be
She likes to dance, she likes to twirl
She loves that old material
At times it may be tough to talk
But this shy little thing can really rock

Some say she takes them back in time
When rock and roll was in its prime
The past is what she listens to
She sings those songs and makes them new
She may find it tough to talk
But this shy little thing can really rock

Champions' brought her back to sing
An original song called "Pretty Little Thing"
Ten competed on that day
Her third place showed she's on her way
Like a lion on the stage
Rock and Roll unlocks her cage
Although she finds it tough to talk
This shy little thing can really rock

About the Author

Rick Ward grew up in the Sacramento area playing football, basketball, and baseball and was named Most Athletic upon graduation from Rio Americano High School in 1975. To be able to play high school sports Rick avoided doctors because he was diagnosed with Juvenile Rheumatoid Arthritis and Ankylosing Spondylitis while in the eighth grade. He kept his condition secret throughout high school and by the time his senior year began he was playing with a very swollen right knee and a Baker's cyst behind that knee. Although his condition make it difficult to run he never missed a game his senior year and was given Honorable Mention honors in football and played for the Sacramento High School Basketball All Stars in the Optimist game. It was during that game the cyst finally ruptured and Rick was hospitalized. Tests taken confirmed the earlier diagnosis and doctors told him he could no longer play sports due to his condition.

Against medical advice, Rick began playing college football and was the fastest player on the team, but his knee swelled and he had to have surgery forcing him to give it up. Rick got the same result later starting to play college basketball and was left to play intramural sports on one good leg. At that point Rick took up the sport of tennis and played on days when his knees felt better. Rick developed his game quickly and within a few years secured a position as the Assistant Pro at the Cameron Park Country Club working under Jeff Hawkins who was a great mentor. Because of his medical condition he would have to give up playing and focus on teaching and got his certification with the United States Professional Tennis Association. During his time at the Cameron Park Country Club Rick began writing tennis newsletters and other free lance articles for a number of publications including "On Court." It was during this time that he began writing poetry and eventually won a poetry award presented to him by the legendary actor, Vincent Price. He wrote poetry off and on during his 20 plus years teaching tennis but eventually had to retire from teaching due to his arthritic condition. During that career he would garner local, regional, and national awards for his work. His introduction at the United States Tennis Association's National Award ceremony is included. For his career work in tennis the USTA flew Rick back to the US Open in New York where they gave him the honor of sitting in the President's Box.

Rick would go back to school and finish his college education by earning undergraduate degrees in both psychology and political science as well as an undeclared minor in journalism. Other health problems made it difficult to work so Rick would go on to complete Masters degree in criminal justice. He would end up doing part time work as a disability counselor and a disability analyst and the topics for his poetry became more about social justice issues such as sexual assault victimization, disability rights, racism, homelessness, and wrongful convictions. Rick continues to give wrongful conviction presentations locally to make people more aware of the problem.

Outside of tennis, Rick has stayed involved with sports organizing recreational activities for a local church, the YMCA, and the Junior Giants. He got back on the tennis court for the last time coaching a local high school tennis team until the pandemic arrived.

Rick is married to Susan Stegenga, who is a former teacher, writer, and editor and has published a number of children's books. Together they have managed a bed and breakfast together and since they are both animal lovers have taken care of many animals for people in the Sacramento area. They are actively involved in advocating for all who face adversity.

Printed in the United States
by Baker & Taylor Publisher Services